DERRYBEG
AND BACK

Other books by John P. McNamee

Donegal Suite
Diary of a City Priest
Clay Vessels and Other Poems
Endurance: The Rhythm of Faith

"In McNamee's Celtic twilight, there is glimmer enough for him to see some terrible beauty amid the shambles of that desolate urban neighborhood where he lives and works."
— *America*

"McNamee, in short, is a poet of the glimpse, but in his words the glimpse takes on sacramental meaning."
— *Commonweal*

"Reading these poems aloud releases the rough quiet of the Irish coast that McNamee has trapped between the words."
— *Sojourners*

"With its seemingly casual rhymes and assonance, this is very well-crafted verse."
— *Philadelphia Inquirer*

"McNamee evokes the peaceful tranquility of Ireland."
— *Publishers Weekly*

DERRYBEG AND BACK

by
John P. McNamee

Dufour Editions

*To Ed Hallinan —
Late for your
birthday but with
Christmas ♡
J McNamee
2010*

First published in the United States of America, 2010
by Dufour Editions Inc., Chester Springs, Pennsylvania 19425

ISBN 0-8023-1347-7 • Paperback (978-0-8023-1347-8)
ISBN 0-8023-1348-5 • Hardcover (978-0-8023-1348-5)

Cover photo by Eugene Martin

On Meeting Dan Berrigan at 30th Street Station was
previously published in *America*

Ocean Morning and *Derrybeg Evening* were
previously published in *Philadelphia Poets 2010*

Library of Congress Cataloging-in-Publication Data

McNamee, John P., 1933-
  Derrybeg and back / by John P. McNamee.
     p. cm.
  ISBN-13: 978-0-8023-1348-5 (hardback)
  ISBN-10: 0-8023-1348-5 (hardback)
  ISBN-13: 978-0-8023-1347-8 (pbk.)
  ISBN-10: 0-8023-1347-7 (pbk.)
 1. Donegal (Ireland : County)--Poetry. I. Title.
  PS3563.C388364D47 2010
  811'.54--dc22

                                        2010027304

Printed and bound in the United States of America

Table of Contents

Derrybeg Beach County Donegal

From the concrete pier out into the water
the huge reinforcing boulders of a bulkhead
look like the endless granite of Donegal
tumbling down to contain the sea as though
to say: *thus far and no farther.*

Feeling the cold wind belting me
I am about to turn landwards until
two wains about four or five run past me
barefoot in tee shirts and shorts

buckets in hand they scamper out
onto the rocks surefooted as mountain goats
scratching from the slippery wet stones
barnacles sea snails whatever.

I don't know because when one asks me:
"What do they eat?" putting kelp into his bucket
I answer: "I don't know!"

Concerned by their lack of caution
I look about for a father a mother.
No one. For now I am the angel of that
childhood image of a winged creature hovering
over two children on a shaky bridge.

Out of nowhere a woman appears
pushing a pram with still another charge.
"These your fellows?" I ask
"They are" her answer.

My duty done. I resume my walk.

Derrybeg Evening

The short quiet man wears the brown
of a day cutting turf in the bog
moist loam covers his hands and shoes
face even   above a soiled work shirt

the chill on him needs whiskey
a "wee Jamie" in hot water with a slice
of lemon spiked with cloves   a drink
that warms like nothing else

but here he is on the stoop outside
a store along a shoulderless road
that passes through a stretch of
houses that are the town

either side of him a child
a girl and a boy   his children
or grandchildren eating away at
his treat of ice cream cones

they seem here on foot
I hope he has them safe home soon
and manages the women so that he
is quickly off to the closest pub.

Swan

On a back street a glimpse
of Dublin before the glass towers

a small stream   now with low tide
little more than a muddy ditch

in the muck a solitary swan
elegant and poised

reaching and pecking   transforming
tidal leavings into ivory down

The Tailor's House

Derrybeg, County Donegal
In memory of Archbishop Lawrence Burke, S.J.,
of Kingston, Jamaica and many pleasant conversations
with him at The Tailor's House

Intermittent conversation
allows the two of us
the leisure of a view
that deserves the hour

John Diver points toward
the cloud hiding the top
of Errigal and comments
on the coming weather

his and Mary Jo's turf land
lie in the bog back there
impossible to reach through
the briars and rhododendron

crowning this early summer
evening after a day of sun
and rain and sun again

here by the road out from
the house which he tends
in her absence we talk of
the Gaeltacht   the effort

to keep the Irish tongue alive
among the young   exposed
day and night to television

before us   more bog
reaching out to the water
first the harbor with small
anchored boats here and there

then the islands   some inhabited
year round   others now just with
holiday homes   lights here
and there on both

we talk of the collapse of
the fishing industry
the flagging tail of the Celtic
Tiger reaching as far as

this outpost of fuchsia and
heather and the smell
of turf warming homes
even on a summer evening

John, I ask: *in the offing there,*
is it the Atlantic or the North Sea?
A man who sees this stark beauty
daily answers: *It's one or the other!*

The Dalmatian Coast

For Gordon and Joan Cavanaugh

Zadar   Pula   Split   Dubrovnik
names from the last century
erupting into ethnic cleansing
unleashed by the death of ideology

from the sea a string of chalk-like
pearls set in cypresses
al fresco crowded markets
shaded by umbrella pines

Now full recovery   as though
the destruction never was
an old castle room frames
a mortar wound for tourists

Now Serb and Croatian children
share classrooms   books
maps that chart new borders
in the back hills   enmity contained

Can the students and their teachers
pull off a turnabout: blur the borders
teach the parents

Beauty captivates the flesh
To obtain permission to enter the soul

                                    --Simone Weil

As still   as attentive
as an old camera
with a panoramic lens
I am a time exposure
not tiring of the expanse

of ocean entering bay
through the Golden Gate
filling harbors where ships
wait the tidal turnaround which
they will ride out to sea

inside at table with pencil and
blank page   mindful of how
these images   now within me
want to come out

Unitarian Church
Providence, Rhode Island

Austere and inviting   imageless
inside   where translucent amber windows with
panels trimmed in a pale red soften the bare walls
under a perfect dome with the reddish-brown of
the tree-lined streets of this late October afternoon

even the air inside breathes an ochre
the Mystery honored without images
or endless words that would undress
and name what in the end is without a name

audiatur altera pars   let another tradition in
these New England freethinkers not wanting
to be told what they are to believe

the massive pulpit seems out of place
so high up   it shows an impulse at work
to pontificate even here   where
an empty silence is the whole point and
less really is more

Diner Breakfast

The *pas de deux* of waitresses
pick-up station to counter has an elegance
that makes my morning paper impossible

"the toast with your eggs, Hon, dark?,"
I nod a quick "yes"
she adds: "for rye, people say: 'burn it!' "

Back again   she is elbows-on-counter
face-in-hands attentive to a ragged old man
who must have the same story every day

Her courtesy to him a kindness
I can take with me all of today

The Solitary Life

(1) Morning

What's the point of it?
At 75 I have to
make a point of it

get up   huddled in bedclothes
sit   thumbs touching   eyes lowered
not looking in or out

get a handle on desire
which goes nowhere
learn to live with longing

longing is not having
and beauty is beholding from afar
not possessing

(2) Noon

Acedia   the noonday devil
the Desert Fathers called
these late morning hours

between early easy beginnings
and the effort to get about something or other
by way of work

whatever needs doing
we want to stay with leisure
surrender to inertia

the sure cure is getting on with it
knowing the day is only half spent
the remaining hours need substance
if nothing else the tasks awaiting
can be distraction from self
which is the point of meditation

(3) Evening

Something dark and bitter
my order at the bar   since
in the dim light I can't read

the twenty some beers chalked
on the blackboards either side
a mute television above the mirror

*"Old Engine Oil" sounds like
what you want* says the barmaid in
jeans she makes designer jeans

Sounds good to me the fellow
beside me comments as he digs
into his huge serving of fries

on this miserable February night
of snow becoming rain becoming
snow for my two-block walk home

I am comfortable here
when alone I prefer bar service
the special is served with

knife and fork wrapped
in a cloth napkin
an elegance of the working class

more spontaneous   less anxious
to impress than the pretense
of downtown restaurants

Another? the barmaid asks
my nod says *yes*   one more
for the road   the walk home

Counter Companion

In another life   a scholar
bending over old documents
or an executive in a downtown
club reading *The Financial Times*

two seats away
quiet as a monk at meditation
with the crossword puzzle of the morning
newspaper   pencil steady as a surgeon's scalpel

wide suspenders over a flannel shirt
neatly tucked into pleated trousers
I have him a longtime widower
this routine his daily escape
from an empty row house

no sadness surrounds him
quiet acceptance that one or
the other goes first   he lives in
the overflow of earlier years

children and grandchildren his comfort
the promised Hundredfold even here
check in hand   puzzle finished
he will enjoy the walk home.

Glasses

Aging and the inevitable eye examinations
prescriptions fittings frames
needing them now for reading, I keep them
everywhere   bedside desktop car shirt pocket
so often lost misplaced or dismembered
I buy them by the half-dozen in dollar stores

Now sunglasses as well
(having been warned about cataracts)
overlooking the river I need them against the glare
to undo the squint   allow the smile that Zen wants

Yet with October the shades are off
to see *au naturel* the hues and tints of the
flaming maples those burning birthday
candles of another autumn

Writing

Not enough   the screen and keyboard
needing an over-sized blank page
shaping the words on paper
with wide margins for glosses

In hand not a pen but
a mechanical pencil that
keeps a fine point and
has an eraser   my mindfullness
of fallibility

Always wanting it better
walking away when the muse
withdraws   wondering whether
she was ever there at all

Sitting

Eyes open   breath minding
as though the in and out is
just air flow   nothing of mine

an ordinary brick wall
across a street   framed in a window
will do for a koan

withering leaves cling hopelessly
against a cold autumn wind
before vanishing into winter

a mirror of my mind running
nowhere with passing thoughts
as fragile as the random leaves

what abides is the self
which also needs leaving

Indian Summer

All the traditions recommend
this straight-sitting   mind clearing
hour especially pleasant here
by the ocean in late autumn

Pleasant!   Teresa of Avila tells how
she would shake her hour glass
to hurry the sand along

Methods vary:
eyes closed has my mind run
like a television screen
that won't shut off

Visual   I prefer the cloudless
empty sky framed in a wreath
of fading scrub pines still

laced with the orange blossoms
of trumpet vines   a flourish of
floral music announcing morning

Breath

The southern wall
a thick thermal pane window
halved by a horizontal bar

Two views:
up close and below
the river shimmering in sunlight

reflecting a restless mind
wanting to leave the surface
dwell *de profundis*

straight out   the spreading city
busy streets steam and smoke
from distant refineries

my measured breathing
one with them
one with the working world

First Light

Between eye blinks
morning paints a hundred
never-to-be repeated skyscapes
luminous swipes as long
as the horizon

Between the streaks
furrows   too dark and dense
to catch any color   more like
the leaden lines of stained glass

giving the lambent stripes
of orange   yellow and a faint red
the look of a Georges Roualt print

River View

Trim as a glazier's knife
a small power boat silent in the distance
cuts water still as a mirror

The wake spreads like folds of
precious cloth   a bridal veil
for the noon nuptials of sun and river

Dancing Colors

A momentary catch of morning
mirrored on the river   from
a sun-yellow   sky-and-sea-blue
mural on the corrugated siding
of an old river pier

Phosphorescent   granulated
so vivid   so intense   that looking for
the same next morning was of no avail
same siding   same colors
but not the luminescence of

yesterday's instant   not some
inner experience just a sudden catch
of what is always out there:
The beauty of the world

Celibacy Again

Many a time I wish I were other
than I am   I weary of the solemn
tides   of the little fields   of this
brooding isle   I long to be rid
of the weight of duty   to have
my part in ampler life

Down a thousand years this lament
of a Scottish monk sounds in another
monk   Benedictine Basil Hume
Abbot   Archbishop   Cardinal
English Order of Merit, etc., etc.

Early on at Westminster
from BBC World Service Radio
a question to the arriving Prelate
Whether he would have liked to marry:
Yes, I would. Did he think about it often?
Yes   his answer   *everyday!*

Monastery Visit

Refectory   4:00 AM

The room   the hour
the dim recessed lighting
that will soon be unnecessary

the grain and gloss of this table
fruit and flowers on a nearby hutch
together yet apart with others at coffee

an hour when as the Irish say
the morning has gold in its mouth
even prayer words would be an interruption

Refectory   6:00 AM

Wanting   needing nothing
nowhere to be   nothing
to do but notice the compulsions
that surface with daylight

content to taste the coffee
choose a spread for the thick bread
possess the day before the day possesses me

Prayer Walk   3:00 PM

A maze   a spiral path
through native grass and flora
carefully recovered and tended

perhaps life   like this labyrinth
goes nowhere but within   with
whatever engages us *en route*
the riverbank farther on is more inviting
downstream a city glows with night and
people whose lives flow in and out of mine

Soup Kitchen

Styx and Lethe together
a street wet with melting snow
a mist of manhole cover steam
and elevated trains roaring above

stores shuttered last night with roll-
down corrugated steel beneath signs:
dollar store   pawn shop   used appliances

The oblivion works both ways:
the street people soon out this Sunday morning
have long drowned all memory or sense of normalcy

The commuters passing overhead
hardly notice this underworld
helpers here on a service project
or a semester break can by Saturday
leave this week behind them

The Badlands

Merciful the sullen sky
the sun would be a surgery lamp
exposing weeping sores

The one lived-in house here padlocked
windows and doors by steel grates
as sure a fire hazard as life on the street

Merciless the closing of another Catholic school
a refuge   a safe house for decades
no consultation   no recourse

Like the abandonment after Katrina:
a physician assuring her poor hospital patients
that they will be rescued

discovers to her dismay that the poor know better:
no helicopters here   as Leon Bloy said:
Money is the blood of the poor.

Uptown Morning

The curb sign reads *Arterial Route*
and means no parking   morning or
early evening   or any hour when
snow is expected

The passing cars are commuters
speeding to downtown offices
as I stand here with a friend
waiting for the methadone clinic to open

A world I tumbled into years ago
because the friend had a delinquent
account and I have what they
call up here   *deep pockets*

We move up in line
put our delinquent dollars down
move along for the paper cup
another morning

Tomorrow another friend
another crisis   it's all quite simple
being here   the only answer to
the question   *and who is my neighbor?*

Recovery House

We have all known the long loneliness
and we have learned that the only solution is
love and that love comes with community
                                    Dorothy Day 1952

The weight of my place descends on me
as I return from a day away
phone messages   someone sick   a funeral
parents wanting redress for a school incident.

A traffic stop is pause enough to
catch the brothers out for a break between sessions
coffee in one hand   cigarette in the other
(one addiction at a time).

Under a doorway sign *Brotherhood Mission*
their banter tells their comfort one with another
and with the shelter and their daily circle
better here than alone on the street.

The traffic light changes and I move on
life has me a lone ranger   yet with the brothers
who have one another   I should count the many
who prop me up back at my place.

Suburban Courtroom

We are in the enemy camp   ignored
sidebar murmers   calendar adjustments
keep us ninety minutes late

as though the time spent waiting will
by delay keep the poor from further
trouble which their number here shows
is their special talent.

Finally the shackled defendants appear
across that all-important rail
their slouched friend beside me heeds
my whispered warning to remove his cap.

The detailed questions from attorneys
have the rawness of pornography
whatever the outcome the plaintiff
will carry her trauma lifelong.

Alleged assailants and plaintiff
everybody loses   the young defendants
face up to twenty years   by all
accounts more criminal upon release

Federal Complex

The new red brick government buildings
are no match for the massive Greek Revival
the *civic excess* of another century

A hint of that tradition survives in a *stoa*
two stories high circling one plain box
the peristyle of an ancient Greek temple

soon becomes the refuge of the homeless
with their blankets, bags and borrowed
shopping carts   a shelter for the night

Your tax dollars at work   making an image
of what government should be about
a message for public servants entering daily

Until the fence went up   the refuge under lock
and key at night   with day   security keeps the
space empty   antiseptic even

Sunday Morning

Words alone won't do
for this strange emptiness
of the early hours downtown

The loneliness of that solitary
counter customer at coffee
framed in a shop window
an Edward Hopper painting

Perhaps the Mystery sought in church
is off there as well   "the presence of absence"
it has been called: the sense that someone
left the room as we were entering

Here we have the new Druids
runners   walkers   bikers
uniform in their spandex vestments

Sunday Morning Coming Down
a troubadour's hymn to the family ritual
of Sunday breakfast   the smell of bacon
coming from open windows   afterwards

the weekly news specials provide
a domestic church by way of television
with politics as a modern faith

In the suburbs full parking lots at malls
for worship on the Sabbath before
an afternoon or evening of football liturgy

More quietly the art museum is open and free
another kind of church   worshippers
seeking beauty as tabernacle of the Good

"Give To Everyone Who Asks of You"

At Irish wakes and weddings
older cousins greet me with
a twenty-dollar bill   hidden
in an embrace or handshake

Refusing or resisting would be
un-Franciscan: *ask nothing   refuse nothing*
and discourteous: the cousins' confidence that
Father will make good use of it

Any protest would expose a clandestine kindness
whose whole intention is to be invisible.
In the funeral homily of one such cousin
I told her children that over the years
she had given me half their inheritance

Days later walking downtown in my Sunday suit
coming from some formal occasion requiring such
I am noticed by a fellow who feigns knowing me
by way of the generic "Father"

Just put on notice from his cleaning job
at the Cathedral behind us: his wife out of work as well
their rental up for sheriff sale etc.

What can I do? I ask
The price of dinner? he answers
out of pocket comes the cousin's twenty
You have received freely   freely give.

Fountain

Ferragosto   Italian for high summer
only mad dogs and Englishmen out
yet the pleasure of morning invites
until the heat requires the asylum
of a store-front air-cooled gallery

Outside again and farther on
the surprise of shade trees   a lawn
benches and flower beds what
the Italians would call a *piazzetta*

A fountain of course   concentric ground-
level water jets fully accessible to children
who laugh and shriek at random squirts
of fish-shaped plumes catching them
in the belly of their tee-shirts

Better than the gallery
this artless art of children teaching us
how to tame summer

Bridge

For Denise Scott Brown and Robert Venturi

As close together as a stand of trees
the downtown towers like humans
show their age by height and skin

Inversely the younger are the taller
the older gray granite   next red brick
then steel   now sleek glass

None have the grace of a bridge
somewhat distant   whose one purpose
is to connect two cities across a river

Twin cables   light and playful as jumping ropes
loop across pylons   descend in an arc to touch
a center span lifting slightly to meet them

Vertical lines spaced like harp strings or music bars
take the symphony to land on either side
the bridge has the achieve of gothic

The illusion of weightlessness
stone mass feather-like in a high vault
there by the work of arch and buttress

Here by cantilever   neither cables nor
harp strings bear the load
side spans support the center and vice versa

By night the loops are lighted according to season
the architects are fond of quoting Augustus Pugin:
Don't construct decoration. Decorate construction!

Korean War Memorial

Two detours   the one now
daily and deliberate through
interfacing granite monoliths
where a large grainy black-and-
white photograph of a foot soldier
heads a litany of local names

Weary   frightened-looking   unshaven
he could be me sixty years ago
he and the others never safe home
I by exemption home safe

Another war was an awakening:
conscientious objectors   deserters
resisters   wanting help from
their religious traditions
that was slow coming

My detour now to remind me
of that unaware earlier bypass
the deferment that dimmed conscience
kept me slow learning

Foreign Film
Majid Majidi's *The Song of Sparrows*

Iran   for years
our pawn   now a problem
wanting weapons we have
but they should not

Away from headlines
threats   stand-offs
resolutions   diplomacy
another story:

A worker on an ostrich ranch
chasing   lassoing   catching
his dancing birds
loses one and thus his job

Wife and family mean a search
countryside to Tehran on his
battered motor bike which by
accident becomes a taxi

Life becomes a back and forth
village to city   with stealth for
not having a cab license nor knowing
directions for his fares

City scrap provides refuse still
precious at home   discarded doors
television parts   loaded impossibly
on a motor bike

The improvisations of a peasant
lost ostriches   overloaded bike
family love   away from the headlines
life goes on

Technology

Hardly a notice that would distract
but what are these huge skeletal steel
structures that seem half-finished
storage tanks among the many of
the refinery yards?

For some minutes now the setting
sun is caught in this cage as in
a lobster pot contained   trapped
packaged like a consumer product.

Nature harnessed   was the romance
of the Industrial Revolution
the vision of *The Detroit Industry* fresco
cycle of muralist Diego Rivera.

The minutes pass   the sun slips below
its enclosure   disappears until morning
even cyberspace lives under other spheres
and orbits   the cosmic mystery of Dante:
L'amor che muove il sole e l'altre stelle.

Airport

A weave of interstates   off and on ramps
approach roads   signs: *arrivals or departures*
a paved meadow of a thousand cars

Sixty years ago nothing but a control tower
and a box of a building little more than a shelter
for passengers out of the weather

Back then a Sunday afternoon family drive
brought us as close as a cyclone fence
noses inserted to watch take-offs and landings

Now so many terminals and gates interconnecting
that the old box if still there is lost in a maze of
multi-level parking lots lacking any center

A mirror of our situation: no grand plan
no overview   random events
we stumble along   cope by improvisation

Migrant Workers

Visible for an instant when a broad-brimmed
straw hat bobs up in the endless green rows
of a treeless field

Up from an impossible up and down daylong
squat among the bushes   the day's wage
measured by the bucket

Indocumentados   many
away from family   sending their few
new dollars home by costly exchange

We connect most of all by indirection:
moist lettuce   plump berries   bright tomatoes
in air-cooled markets distant from the scorching fields

The Ides of March

Even the twice-daily tide
drowning a decaying river pier
cannot by that watering sustain
through winter the weeds

that found root in the rotting
railroad ties and wind-caught soil.
The straw-like bushes are as brittle
and finished as anything dead.

Hard to imagine that before
the month is out these remnants
will green and grow

Here and now   a week
still in the fist of winter
that seems as unlikely as
impossible as Easter

Ocean Morning

Like the ripe yolk of a breakfast egg
bruised by a wedge of toast
dawn spills orange across the water

until the morning loses color as
sea and sky play mirrors with a glare
forcing my eyes landwards

where the light brightens
the vinyl siding of new seashore homes
a yellow   bright as butter

and royal blue gables against a paler sky
as though the houses want
their own play with the new day.

Builders

The overlay of human on cosmic
has me here again   wrapped in bedclothes
on the second-floor deck of a beach-
house waiting for the sun which will
appear on schedule at ten past seven

I wait as well for the parade of cars
vans and pickup trucks of workmen arriving
for another day of measuring
climbing   hammering and sawing
at new houses going up off season

I hope these workers see themselves as I do
who envy everything about them:
their skills   their balance on a slanted roof
the quiet   punctuated by the sound of power tools
the glide of gulls curious about lunch pails

Cooler weather and the progress of the work
will soon have them inside where they can still
see the beach   the breakers   the migrating birds
following the coastline   all this still visible
outside the unfinished empty windows

Moods

Between this house and the inlet
sand dunes thick with briars dark and unfriendly
in the shadows of early morning

By late afternoon the scrub pines and bushes
are more inviting as the failing sun penetrates
the spaces between shrubs and thickets

Strange how our connection to surroundings
depends upon the play of shadow and light
we can be as fragile as the tall reeds
which will not survive the winter

Migrations

The spilling of ocean into inlets and bays
must confuse these small dark birds
now a hundred black specks   furious
on the deck outside this window

they seem lost   anxious
about to begin running into one another
overall instinct will guide them
more surely than thought guides me

Beauty

The practice has seminary origins
a stretch as stark and dry as this driftwood
wizened by wind and sun   on

this beach where I often try something
which might be prayer: I gaze on
breakers crashing on a jetty as a metaphor.

Surviving those early years by forcing
life into the mind   a bypass of emotion
never crying   ever   more like

a silent gaze before a masterpiece
when alone in a church or museum
a Greek statue   Chartes   Cézanne

On Meeting Dan Berrigan at 30th Street Station

Up from the underground in Philadelphia
easier now than that appearance years ago
a Methodist church   the Feds in hot pursuit
the task the same   a word   the Word
in and out of season
I don't know why the Bishops have
to go to the State Department to get
help in reading the New Testament.

A smile when he sees me   a familiar face
an embrace   a nod in the great hall
to the giant sculpture   an angel of mercy
                        embracing a war victim
a coffee   and off   most times
a Quaker or college or Catholic Worker place
(why never a mainstream Catholic church?)
I am trying to get with a much bigger
thing than this little churchy thing
which has been proposed as a real thing.

En route we pass an empty place   once
Fellowship House.   I recall a night thirty
years ago as though yesterday.   Another
talk and then a too self-conscious question:
Q: Father Dan, what does it mean to be
a priest in this Vatican II Church?

A: Well, Father, I haven't thought about
that sort of thing in a long time.
(pause)
I don't know. Perhaps we should stop
thinking how we are different and
think how we are the same as others.
(longer pause)
I think we should get rid of all that
sacred language we use to talk about ourselves.
(again, pause)

I don't know, Father, perhaps it means
being with and for other in ways the
authorities would call irresponsible.

We arrive. The coffee spurt wanes. The task begins.
After all the years still an eager audience,
young and old wanting encouragement,
strength,   comfort,   wisdom,   direction,
more than one man can give with one night
or the economy of the long haul.
It is a terrifying thing to shoulder
the hope of others especially
                    when they have ceased to hope
                    for themselves at all.

The message   whether early on in Germantown
or now   has that Gospel madness:
"This is a hard saying.   Who can hear it?"
Understand that it is not God who will beat
swords into plowshares; it is yourselves.
It is you, . . . Disarm. It must be done
and it cannot be done. And if it is to be
done, it must be done by God; and it must
be done by us.

Most will not.   Most cannot.   The sure return to
classroom   parish   family
The "normalizing" of faith by normal times into a
mere intellectual consent can only be considered
as a curse of God. Faith is abnormal, in the sense
that it acts most truly in crisis and dislocation. . .

So. The word returns to the preacher. His burden
heavier for his hearing it again more clearly
than his listeners: "The sower went forth to sow."
All he can do. One frail man goes home weighed
down by his impossible task. The Mystery of Weakness:
Saint Paul Franz Jaeggerstaetter the Salvadoran Martyrs.

My brother and I stand like the fences
of abandoned farms, changed times
too loosely webbed against
deicide homicide
A really powerful blow, a cataclysm
would bring us down like scarecrows.

But before the return   some comfort
a party: old friends   a bracer
(or two).   Endless talk and late to bed
the warmth of a wayside inn:
Night falls. The sleepy fire sputters, ruminates
like a dreaming dog.
Bones shift in sleep. One red eye
closes like a log.

Late to rise.   Off at noon.
Returning to the train a hospital stop
The visitation of the sick
with all else a Corporal Work of Mercy.
These many beautiful days
Cannot be lived again. . .
I take them in full measure.

Devil's Advocate

Remembering Richard McSorley, S.J.

Thrusts and parries
our banter took the form of fencing
pressing him to his predictable conclusions.

The duel had a serious side:
taking a truth to its contrary
to see whether it can still be true.

Dick, I would ask: *how can we*
feed the hungry   defend ourselves
save the planet from over-population?

His response as unhesitating
as his original lunge:
We are not told to survive   but to love.

Embedded

Starting with Iraq
a casual word takes
on new meaning

bravely enough journalists
insert themselves among
combat troops   soon

niceties appeared
patriotism   camaraderie
drown   *the blood-red tide*
truth the first victim of war

then network news
foreign and domestic are as replays
officials with expected answers if any

guests are almost never a Howard Zinn
Michael Moore dismissed as an entertainer
never a Noam Chomsky

here the media are embedded not in combat
but in culture   *whoever discovered water
you can be sure it wasn't a fish*
said Marshall MacLuhan

American Exceptionalism is the message
the need for Pablo Neruda as antidote:

*They speak to me of Venezuelas
Chiles and Paraguays;
I don't know what they are talking about
I only know the skin of the earth
 which has no name*

**Philip Berrigan's Funeral Mass
Compared to the Air We Breathe**

Who but Hopkins could make a poem from air?
*This air, which, by life's law, My lung must draw and draw
Now but to breathe its praise, Minds me in many ways*

Of faith. Most days now faith seems draining from me
like steam thinning into air from my morning kettle.
Along with my weakness I count my plight the drain
of times when, it seems, many have put aside belief.

Faith as air. That noontime in church
Nestling me everywhere,
…My more than meat and drink, My meal at every wink;
No righteous claiming what others lack   no invoking faith
in face of loss   just there

Like air. *Do but stand Where you can lift your hand
Skywards: rich, rich it laps around the fourfinger gaps*
Not like my kettle losing steam to air   No, open church
doors and we streaming in breathed faith from Phil's
absent presence in a pine box   relic and reliquary
in the finest Catholic sense, *a needful, never spent
and nursing element.*

Crowded into pews and overflowing onto floor
we were those hours breathing one another's air
no, breathing faith from each other.   One fails and
tears start, someone near is comfort.   Or the singing
"Lamb of God," say, invites all away from grief.
I say that we are wound with mercy round and round.

A mercy Brother Daniel's words, understated as befits
faith: "We see only obscurely…" yet we reach.
A stretch more grace than reach: "Where Christ in
Phil's ordeal?" With us as promised: "where two or three
gather…" in family 'round him, in caregivers, in peacemakers

Now bringing bread and wine and – I had to look twice –
hammers! Young Davids intent on Goliath   intent on
keeping on with Phil gone. Faith *This one work has to do –
Let all God's glory through.*

This Mass a grace to my more than Advent emptiness
Advent lights are not bright Christmas skies and angel choirs
more the small candle framed in a winter window
the pinlight of the Magi star against a midnight sky
Even in absence Philip such a presence and makes,
*O marvellous! New Nazareths in us, where she shall yet
conceive Him, morning, noon, and eve; New Bethlems,
and He born There, evening, noon, and morn.*

Ray Kane (1923-1993)

Father Mac,
Something that will turn
the medals into plowshares

Joan   that transformation happened
with each wedding   six daughters
bride   or bridesmaid   in turn
each solo with your father

Daddy's little girl   the ritual dance
at table with mother and brothers
we saw the alchemy at work
knew he had brought the war home

Saw more   the miracle
love   forgiving   understanding   overcoming
Merrill's Marauder   never wore the medals
too many for his lean chest

Purple Heart   Bronze Star   Presidential Unit
Emblem   Honorable Service World War Two
Asiatic-Pacific Campaign Medal with
Four Service Stars   Etc.   Etc.

No medals for the malaria   typhus   dysentery
more often than he could remember
wet   muddied   hungry in the jungle
few of them survived

In the close world of parish school
you and your sister Kathleen met a brother
and a sister who recognized your name:
Your Dad carried our Dad half way across China

Deeper than the wound that won a Purple Heart
his anguish over killing   to discover on the man
a photo of his own wife and two children
remorse he took with him to the grave

His medals became plowshares with you
your testimony before Congress against
a draft for Vietnam and again your training
to counsel conscientious objectors

Your own brother an early candidate
your Dad gave you that Purple Heart
in approval and appreciation claiming that
recruiters would never have your brothers

I remember him in later years
this man of brothers priests and sisters nuns
across the room at family gatherings
removed   but gracious   a hint of a smile

All of us spread out on chairs and floor
children and spouses   grandchildren
all ages   too many to count   a comfort
to him needing that comfort

After Mass I would say to no one but myself
Next time Ray should do the homily
this man knows more of life and death
than the rest of us together.

Intercessions

The comment of a friend:
every mass the same weary litany
Iraq   Afghanistan   Haiti
Darfur and all of Africa

Because we must not see our place
and lives as a center which is
in fact out beyond us all
a space measured by our bombs

which because of distance we never hear
the Eucharist is always for everybody
the priest should extend his arms widely
as though embracing the whole world

Local Boy

One could call the choices
gravity or a lack of imagination
high school   then seminary
at either end of the same highway
both a short walk from home

Now my morning watch these many years
ends with the lights and roar of a truck
emptying one then a second disposal bin
in the cul-de-sac beneath my bedroom window
but not before an imaginary stretch out that

window would see my birthplace hospital
on the same street just downtown
"Mac, you haven't come far in life"
Comfort comes from the much-traveled
Dag Hammarskjöld: *The true journey is within.*

Author Biography

For over 25 years Fr. John McNamee worked in an inner-city parish of his native Philadelphia. He helped transform a deteriorating church with a destitute elementary school and a run-down rectory into a thriving parish at the heart of its community. His efforts on behalf of the poor include returning a Catholic Worker house to Philadelphia and organizing Catholic Peace Fellowship/Pax Christi.

He has received numerous awards and honors including The Adela Dwyer, St. Thomas of Villanova Peace Award, 1994; The American Catholic Historical Society's John Barry Award, 2002; the Cardinal O'Hara Service Award from the Notre Dame Club of Philadelphia, 2005; the Bread & Roses Community Fund Paul Robeson Award for Lifetime Achievement and dedication to peace and justice issues, 2008; the Humanitarian Award from Neumann University; and honorary Doctorates from Villanova University and the University of Scranton.

He has written two previous collections of poetry and his autobiography, *Diary of a City Priest* was made into a film starring David Morse as John McNamee. He retired in 2008 but still remains active in social justice issues as well as in the local Philadelphia community where he worked for so many years.